Once Upon a Sushi Cat

Once Upon a Sushi Cat

THE MYSTERY AND THE MAGIC

**TANGE & NAKIMUSHI PEANUTS
AND SAM STALL**

RUNNING PRESS
PHILADELPHIA

Manufactured under license from Yellow Brain Co, Ltd.

Running Press
Hachette Book Group
1290 Avenue of the Americas, New York, NY 10104
www.runningpress.com
@Running_Press

Printed in China

First Edition: September 2020

Published by Running Press, an imprint of Perseus Books, LLC, a subsidiary of Hachette Book Group, Inc. The Running Press name and logo is a trademark of the Hachette Book Group.

The Hachette Speakers Bureau provides a wide range of authors for speaking events. To find out more, go to www.hachettespeakersbureau.com or call (866) 376-6591.

The publisher is not responsible for websites (or their content) that are not owned by the publisher.

Print book cover and interior design by Jenna McBride.

Library of Congress Control Number: 2020932650

ISBNs: 978-0-7624-9735-5 (hardcover), 978-0-7624-9733-1 (ebook)

RRD-S

10 9 8 7 6 5 4 3 2 1

Contents

The History of Sushi Cats

The history of sushi cats is no more than the history of mankind itself. Their existence has always been with us—as intimately bound to humanity as wasabi to pickled ginger. Closely tied to human life, they have influenced us since ancient times.

You can see the trail of this history from primitive cave drawings to classical paintings. Some scientists even say that such mystery of age-old culture was created through the magical power of sushi cats itself.

In Japan, there are many myths and old writings that say encounters with sushi cats can bring people good luck. But where did sushi cats come from?

Over the ocean and over the mountains, they were born on Sushi Cat Island, a magical place where cats meet sushi. From this magical place, the sushi cats set forth, traversing our mundane world on their flying plates, spreading happiness and joy.

Mom,

why am I

sushi?

One significant feature of sushi cats is that sightings remain rare and encounters with them are different, depending on time and place.

The most common theory suggests that the chances of spotting a sushi cat depend entirely on one's state of mind. Our consciousness is most attuned to them when we step away from the chaos of our daily life and contemplate, if only for a moment, what lies beyond.

However, the reality of our modern world is that there are few such gaps and pauses in life, which, unfortunately, makes it harder to see sushi cats—yet not impossible. Pause for a moment and look past the minutiae and you just might find a sushi cat looking back at you.

As the well-known saying goes:

Where there are

gaps,

there are

sushi cats.

On the following pages, you'll learn a little bit more about these extremely unusual life-forms and see if you can spot them in their natural habitats. But don't expect lengthy origin stories or detailed explanations of their behavior. To explain sushi cats is to diminish them. Better to simply accept and enjoy and open yourself to the magic and mystery of these ancient mystical creatures.

Meet the Sushi Cats

NYA-TA

Hero of all sushi cats, Nya-ta must bear the challenge of carrying a very angry lobster on his back. He accomplishes this with grace and courage, making him a paragon of patience and nobility.

WA-SA-BI

Wa-sa-bi is a third-generation sushi cat who is always fast to fight. In a scrap, she's just as sharp and formidable as her condiment namesake.

TORO-MI

An idol of everyone, Toro-mi dreams of the future and carries all her possessions in a single, fashionable purse. She knows the wisdom of traveling light, and not becoming overly attached to objects.

MAGGIE

A nagging but caring grandma whose quilting skills win contests, Maggie symbolizes the importance of honoring the past as one strives toward the future.

MARGO

A mischievous and curious girl, Margo works to become as patient and enlightened as her mentor, Nya-ta, not yet realizing that, in order to do so, she must cease her striving, quiet her mind, and understand that the things she seeks are already within.

MIYAO

A strange sushi cat with mysterious powers whose footsteps are always stealthy, Miyao can lift the observer out of the mundane world and into the sushi cat's rarified plane of existence.

MS. LILY

A silver screen actress who once took the world by storm, Ms. Lily enjoyed her time in the spotlight but didn't let it go to her head. Now she's content to live out her days in harmony with the universe.

FEVER

Fever is incomparable—who else would pair a candy-dotted silver garland cape with those shades? He is perhaps the bravest of all the sushi cats, because he has the courage to be his truest self.

LONELY JIMMY

Cold and abandoned, Lonely Jimmy wanders the sushi cat world alone and is greedy when it comes to food. Someday, he will learn that the path to true wealth comes not from seeking but from letting go.

CHIBI

A tiny sushi cat riding a warship of seaweed, vegetables, and flowers, Chibi, though young, already knows that it's important to appreciate the here and now, rather than stress about future unknowns.

EBINOSUKE

The naïve Prince Charming, Ebinosuke found true happiness, realizing that joy comes not from achievements and possessions but from cultivating a quiet, balanced mind.

BOTCHAN

Though born to a well-to-do family, Botchan knows that material wealth is nothing compared to spiritual riches. Instead of flaunting his money, he lives simply, spending his days (and fortune) helping the less privileged.

GERONIMO

A natural athlete, Geronimo excels at many sports and appreciates that those who wish to develop a sound mind must cultivate a sound body as well.

SHAKE-BOO

Shake-boo sports a tie and works hard, but this sushi cat's attitude is as laid-back as his ears. He understands that success isn't the key to happiness; rather, happiness is the key to success.

Spot a
Sushi Cat

Cows placidly graze in a mountain valley, offering an unconditional welcome to the tiny, plated mystical creature in their midst.

Among a bevy of parasols used for shade and concealment, a sushi cat is revealed.

A bench is a useful place for contemplation. No wonder a sushi cat waits there, seeking someone who can spare a moment to notice her.

A tiny wonder waits beside a path through the woods. He'll be found not by the climber intent on reaching the summit, but by the seeker focused on where she is right now.

As boats are for journeys, sushi cats are for journeys of self-discovery.

In such a busy place, will anyone pause long enough to spot the sushi cat?

As we travel the thoroughfares of life, a quick glance to the right or left could yield an astonishing revelation.

What better place for a sushi cat than a mailbox to find a thoughtful soul capable of noticing her?

While waiting for someone to spot him, a sushi cat takes in the world from his rooftop perch.

If one looks down from his meal, one might notice a special treat—not for eating but for contemplation and joy.

All journeys begin with a first step, just as all revelations begin by opening one's mind and seeing what others might miss.

On a crisp, silent morning, a sushi cat waits on a bridge, looking for someone who can span the void between his world and theirs.

This world's felines are well aware of sushi cats. The two separate species don't antagonize each other, but rather cohabit with an attitude of mutual respect and reverence.

While navigating your bustling journey, don't forget to relax and contemplate the here and now.

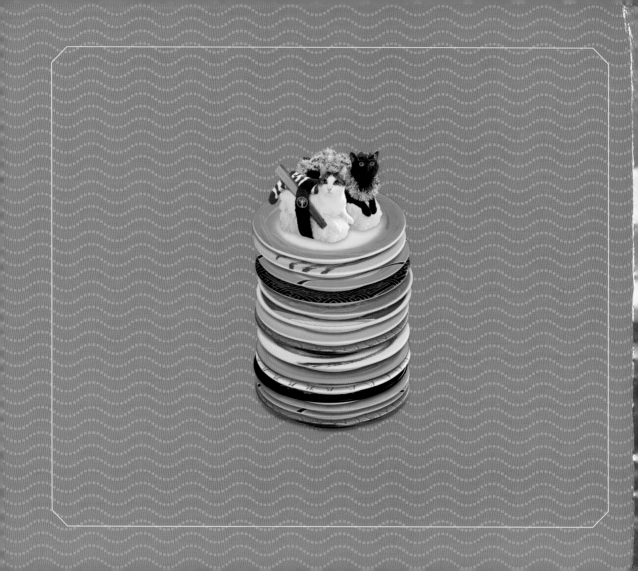